D1001580

Máquinas maravillosas/Mighty Machines

Camiones de basura/Garbage Trucks

por/by Terri DeGezelle

Traducción/Translation: Dr. Martín Luis Guzmán Ferrer
Editor Consultor/Consulting Editor: Dra. Gail Saunders-Smith

Consultor/Consultant: Alice Jacobsohn
Director, Public Affairs and Industry Research
National Solid Wastes Management Association
Washington, DC

Capstone
press

Mankato, Minnesota

Pebble Plus is published by Capstone Press,
151 Good Counsel Drive, P.O. Box 669, Mankato, Minnesota 56002.
www.capstonepress.com

1 2 3 4 5 6 11 10 09 08 07 06

Library of Congress Cataloging-in-Publication Data
DeGezelle, Terri, 1955–
    [Garbage trucks. Spanish & English]
    Camiones de basura = Garbage trucks/de Terri DeGezelle.
    p. cm.—(Pebble plus. Máquinas maravillosas = Pebble plus. Mighty machines)
    Includes index.
    ISBN-13: 978-0-7368-6673-6 (hardcover)
    ISBN-10: 0-7368-6673-6 (hardcover)
    1. Refuse collection vehicles—Juvenile literature. 2. Refuse and refuse disposal—Juvenile literature. I. Title:
Garbage trucks. II. Title. III. Pebble plus. Máquinas maravillosas. IV. Pebble plus. Mighty machines.
TD794.D428518 2007
629.225—dc22   2005037462

Summary: Simple text and photographs present garbage trucks, their parts, and their jobs—in both English
    and Spanish.

Editorial Credits
Martha E. H. Rustad, editor; Katy Kudela, bilingual editor; Eida del Risco, Spanish copy editor; Molly Nei,
    set designer; Ted Williams, book designer; Wanda Winch, photo researcher; Scott Thoms, photo editor

Photo Credits
Capstone Press/Karon Dubke, cover, 7, 9, 11, 13, 15, 21; Corbis/Sygma/Next Photo/Kwok Wing Kuen, 19;
Index Stock Imagery/Elfi Kluck, 17; Index Stock Imagery/Omni Photo Communications Inc., 5; iStockphoto/
Niilo Tippler, 1

The author thanks Mark Hibbs, Engineer, Heil Company, for his assistance with this book.
Pebble Plus thanks Waste Management of Mankato, Minnesota for assistance with photo shoots.

Note to Parents and Teachers

The Máquinas maravillosas/Mighty Machines set supports national standards related to
science, technology, and society. This book describes garbage trucks in both English and
Spanish. The images support early readers in understanding the text. The repetition of
words and phrases helps early readers learn new words. This book also introduces early
readers to subject-specific vocabulary words, which are defined in the Glossary section.
Early readers may need assistance to read some words and to use the Table of Contents,
Glossary, Internet Sites, and Index sections of the book.

Table of Contents

Tabla de contenidos

A Garbage Truck's Job

A garbage truck picks up
and dumps garbage.

Cómo trabaja un camión de basura

El camión de basura

recoge y tira la basura.

5

Garbage Truck Parts

Garbage trucks have
lights that flash.
The lights warn people
to stay out of the way.

Las partes del camión de basura

Los camiones de basura tienen
luces intermitentes. Las luces son
para advertirles a las personas
que se aparten de su camino.

6

lights/luces

Garbage trucks have arms
that pick up garbage cans.
The arms dump the garbage
into the hopper.

Los camiones de basura tienen
unos brazos para levantar
los botes de basura. Los brazos
meten la basura en la tolva.

hopper/tolva

arm/brazo

Garbage trucks have
packing panels.
Packing panels crush
the garbage in the hopper.

Los camiones de basura tienen
unos paneles compresores.
Los paneles aplastan la basura
que está en la tolva.

packing panel/panel compresor

Garbage truck drivers

sit inside the cab.

They push buttons to move

the arm and packing panel.

Los conductores de los camiones

de basura se sientan en la cabina.

Ahí aprietan los botones para mover

los brazos y el panel compresor.

A screen shows drivers
the inside of the hopper.
The screen also helps drivers
back up safely.

Un monitor le permite al conductor
ver el interior de la tolva.
El monitor también ayuda al
conductor a retroceder sin peligro.

screen/monitor

What Garbage Trucks Do

Garbage trucks pick up
garbage around town.
Some trucks pick up items
for recycling too.

Qué hacen los camiones de basura

Los camiones de basura recogen
la basura por toda la ciudad.
Algunos camiones también recogen
objetos para reciclarlos.

Garbage trucks dump
garbage at landfills.
Newspapers, bottles,
and cans are taken
to recycling centers.

Los camiones de basura tiran
la basura en los vertederos.
Los periódicos, las botellas y las latas
los llevan a los centros de reciclaje.

19

Mighty Garbage Trucks

Garbage trucks pick up,

carry, and dump garbage.

Garbage trucks are

mighty machines.

Maravillosos camiones de basura

Los camiones de basura recogen,

transportan y tiran la basura.

Los camiones de basura son

unas máquinas maravillosas.

21

Glossary

flash—to blink on and off

hopper—a container on a garbage truck that holds garbage

landfill—a large area of land where garbage is buried

packing panel—a large, flat piece of metal that crushes garbage tightly in the hopper

recycling—remaking old items such as newspapers, glass bottles, or aluminum cans into new items

warn—to tell a person there may be danger

Glosario

advertir—decirles a las personas que puede haber peligro

intermitente—que se prende y se apaga

el panel compresor—herramienta de metal larga y plana que aplasta la basura y la mete en la tolva

reciclar—utilizar objetos usados como periódicos, botellas de vidrio o latas de aluminio para construir otros objetos

la tolva—recipiente grande del camión donde se mete la basura

el vertedero—terreno muy grande donde se entierra la basura

Internet Sites

FactHound offers a safe, fun way to find Internet sites related to this book. All of the sites on FactHound have been researched by our staff.

Here's how:

1. Visit *www.facthound.com*

2. Choose your grade level.

3. Type in this book ID **0736866736** for age-appropriate sites. You may also browse subjects by clicking on letters, or by clicking on pictures and words.

4. Click on the **Fetch It** button.

FactHound will fetch the best sites for you!

Sitios de Internet

FactHound proporciona una manera divertida y segura de encontrar sitios de Internet relacionados con este libro. Nuestro personal ha investigado todos los sitios de FactHound. Es posible que los sitios no estén en español.

Se hace así:

1. Visita *www.facthound.com*

2. Elige tu grado escolar.

3. Introduce este código especial **0736866736** para ver sitios apropiados según tu edad, o usa una palabra relacionada con este libro para hacer una búsqueda general.

4. Haz clic en el botón **Fetch It**.

¡FactHound buscará los mejores sitios para ti!

Index

Índice